Beach Reads

adrift

THIRD STREET
WRITERS

Laguna Beach, California

Beach Reads 4: Adrift

Editors
Amy Francis Dechary
Rina Palumbo

Poetry Editor
Barbara DeMarco-Barrett

Copy Editor
Candice Yacono

Cover Image
Jennifer Griffiths

Cover Design, Typography, Print Production
Ris Fleming

ISBN-13: 978-0-9970853-9-6

Typeset in Garamond and Copperplate.

The Children of Captain Grant 004 by Édouard Riou
used courtesy of *Wikimedia Commons.*

CONTENTS

PROLOGUE

An Introduction to Adrift

AD

RI

FT

CODA

PROLOGUE

AN INTRODUCTION TO ADRIFT

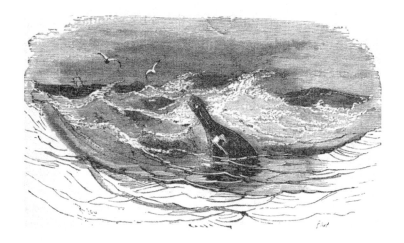

Every Monday, the members of Third Street Writers meet in the community room at the Laguna Beach Library. It's a cheery space, filled with puppets, bottles of glue, and jars of glitter used for Saturday Storytime. It's not a perfect space—the heating vents rattle, and organizing the large tables in the small room is like trying to solve a Rubik's Cube puzzle. But after five years, it's become our refuge, the place where we write together and share our successes and failures.

Last spring, our creative team gathered in our library refuge and landed on the theme of "Adrift" for our fourth *Beach Reads* anthology. "Adrift" had so many possibilities—it brought to mind images of unmoored boats, carefree strolls, and lazy summer days. It was perfect. We eagerly awaited the responses that would come from our contributors. We carried on, business as usual.

Flash forward a year, and nothing is business as usual. COVID-19 has taken over. The doors to our library refuge are locked. Schools, houses of worship, and government offices sit empty and dark. Yellow caution tape closes off our beloved beaches and hiking trails. The beachside cafes and gift shops that are the lifeblood of our quaint tourist town are trying to make ends meet with curbside pickup and online sales. And our vernacular contains a new pandemic vocabulary previously confined to dystopian literature: lockdown, flattening the curve, social distancing. As we shelter in place, we are physically segregated by new boundaries: face masks, Zoom meetings, and X's on grocery store floors. Little feels carefree.

And many of us find ourselves mentally adrift. With old routines gone, we face an uncertain, anxiety-filled future as we strive to maintain our physical safety, economic stability, and interpersonal relationships. Life is marked by confusion over ever-changing rules of what actions and behaviors are safe, over what is allowed. An ever-present fear hangs over us like a cloud.

In many ways, *Beach Reads: Adrift* is a time capsule, a snapshot of pre-COVID life. It shares narratives and images of what used to be: crowded celebrations, travel, university lectures, gym workouts. We dine with a woman searching for a beloved lobster dinner, we climb aboard a train with a father processing personal loss, and we come across an unexpected roadblock during a morning commute. But *Adrift* also highlights the enduring aspects of life that give us hope and joy—the shared experiences that can bring us together. We feel a new mother's love and apprehension at the birth of her first child. We empathize with the bliss and heartbreak of a forbidden love affair. We imagine the thrill of riding atop the perfect Pacific wave.

As we try to find our way through the pandemic, we hope this collection of words and images provides readers with an anchor—a connection with a character, place, or emotion that entertains and inspires—and an understanding that, while we are now adrift in such an unprecedented way, the stories, poems, and art we share will always keep us grounded.

And we wish all our readers good health and happiness.   —AFD & RP

ad

RECALCULATING
BY JAMES BROSCHART

The Earth's magnetic pole drifted
more than thirty miles last year,
like a buoy dragging its anchor.

Seems its shift is increasing.
Migrating birds veer off track.
Turtles wash onto unfamiliar sands.

We'll have to recalculate once again.
Humans need to seek solid ground
as our grip on reality slips.

Of course, we are usually quick to adapt:
we rewrite history when convenient,
toss out our rules of conduct

whenever it suits us. Many
of us are happy to be governed
by the actions of shape shifters.

Let's hope our slippery
magnetic guidepost won't pull
civilization too far off course.

SLUMBER IN SUSPENSION
ALEXANDRA PRADO

IF I LOSE MYSELF AGAIN
BY ANTHONY DIPIETRO

after Eduardo Corral's "Se Me Olvido Otra Vez"

my mind will split itself   two halves never to rejoin
if i can write it   it will not come true

men in black pajamas   battle shadows   kick
their legs   bar their arms   moan like wolves ripped open

my mind will split itself   two halves never to rejoin

chased in my own home   by my father   in red makeup
farmer's pitchfork   devil's trident

if i can write it   it will not come true

thick trunk   stark branch   watch me try to sleep
they can't come in   the blinds are drawn

my mind will split itself   two halves never to rejoin

lightning   ghostly roads   small metal implements
tongues of snakes   my mind my mind my mind   my mind

if i can write it   it will not come true
my mind will split itself   two halves never to rejoin

FISHTAIL BRAID
BY ANNE GUDGER

AFTER MY HUSBAND DIED. After my son was born. And we were a fish braid, swimming on the bottom of the ocean with our fish tails and fish fins and fish gills. With our silver scales muted in the no-light belly of the sea. With fish lips and puffed cheeks. With rust-colored fish eyes that saw sideways and not ahead. Me wrapping fins around my tiny perfect fish boy. His fish heart pulsing with mine. Thrumming. Beating. Beating. Fish mama and fish boy. Swimming and drifting in our fish braid with a blip fish memory. Me remembering the moon. Him only knowing the bottom of the ocean. Me whispering. "I promise to swim us to ocean air and sky and salt and sand. To cheesecloth clouds. To pewter skies. To slow pink sunsets. When my gills and heart are strong enough," I said. "I promise."

Fishtail braid, chevron-shaped, two strands, not three. Two. Like a mermaid tail. Fishtail braids look best messy.

I wish I'd kept your hair.

Grey like steel. Wet concrete. Silver flecks like fish scales. No longer brown like your chestnut beard with cinnamon streaks.

I wish I'd kept a lock big enough to braid a tiny braid. One inch long. Mini bumps of right strands to middle. Left strands to middle. Mini weave. Mini plait. Was your hair long enough? Your hairdresser left a message for you a week after you died: "You missed your appointment. Is everything okay?"

I love the Victorians for keeping their dead beloveds' hair. Something to moor the unmoored. Turn it into jewelry. Death ritual. *Memento Mori* carved in rings, in lockets. Miniature braids of hair woven in 9K gold bands. Initials. Love words. Memory words etched on the insides. To a husband, a wife, a mom, a dad, a child. *Memento Mori:* Remember you must die.

I wish I'd kept your hair.

Short in your man cut. I'd braid a tiny one-inch braid of wooly cloud-colored hair. The steely shade that cautions rain, storm. I'd coil your mini braid in a silver locket with a heart hand carved in the metal. Your initials in fancy script: KLN. Wear it over my heart. Over the boom, boom, swish of me. *Memento Mori.*

I wish I'd kept your hair.

ARROYO SECO 1

DOROTHY ENGLANDER

THE BLUE FLAME
BY LEE THOMAS

IT WAS FRANCISCO Alvadar's final call of the day. Somewhere in the distance he heard bells chime the eleventh hour. The neighborhood lay five miles from his along the 10, but he recognized the little 1940s bungalows, close-set. Cinder blocks littered weedy lawns on side streets. Rusted RVs, their windows obscured by drifts of junk, sat moored like ships along the avenue. No one lived in a rusting hulk by choice, but each day he passed dozens. He'd just come from Beverly Hills, where the housekeeper spoke in hushed Spanish, trying not to wake the household, as he tested the line that ran alongside a new pool large enough to swallow his mother's house. He lived with her, in conditions only slightly better than the RVs, but not for much longer. He almost had the down payment for a studio. He would rent it for a few years until he saved enough for a two-bedroom. Then they would escape together. He couldn't leave her. He was her only child.

He rang the bell of a trim little bungalow, then knocked, conscious of the dark windows like shining eyes all around. He'd been bitten many times by dogs, but he feared people more. Bare-chested men had menaced him when he came to shut off service for nonpayment. He'd endured the tears and tragic stories of countless women. He'd seen a gun only once, which he considered lucky. He'd held up his hands and said, "Amigo," and backed away from the gang-inked boy. Francisco had marked "No Access to Line" and known he would not report it.

The door opened on the chain and an elderly woman peered out, her iron gray hair wild about her face. "You from the gas company?"

"Here to return service."

"Those bastards locked it."

"Notes say a stove leak, Miss—" He consulted his notes. "Miss Nolan."

"You always work so late?"

"I work till the jobs are cleared."

Humph. "Come in." She released the chain.

"You got any dogs? Anyone else in the household?"

"I'm alone."

He preferred old women to young ones. Housewives looked at him hungrily. It wasn't sex, exactly, but some need that ran on a parallel line. They'd lean against the stove to catch his eye. They'd make little jokes, turn up their presence like a flame. They revealed secrets and smiled in ways sad or lonely or both. People think they want something from you, but most people don't know what they want.

First, he found the kitchen at the back and lay on the ground to check the connections to the stove. He smelled for gas, but the cool air hung leaden in the room. Next he went out the back door, the old woman like a dog at his heel. The yard looked cared for, but past tense. She'd given up. The bouncing beam of his headlamp caught a wild spray of bougainvillea, the shaggy dead heads of zinnias. He pitied the old woman, her house overwhelming, her door on the chain. He thought of his mother, waiting up for him as she always did. The prayer candle aglow in the window, she'd sit wrapped in a shawl on the couch where he would lie to sleep in her borrowed warmth.

"Paco, *mi amor*," she'd murmur, kissing his cheek. What would she do without him? He would rescue her to the gleaming apartment with new plumbing and walls of solid cinderblock from which no roaches could swarm. Still, he felt the whisper of lost youth escaping.

"Did anyone service the stove?" he called to the porch.

"What? I'm half-deaf," shouted the woman from her doorway. A dog—vicious, slavering—barked savagely from across the fence. The gasman flinched. He knelt by the meter and checked the pressure from the main, then turned the valve on the house line and heard the invisible surge. He marked the meter and returned to the house.

No scent of gas by the stove. He rose up off the floor, the woman near his elbow. She would be about his mother's age. He turned the first burner and the corpse scent rose.

"Wait," she said. "You have to do it the old-fashioned way." She pulled a box of matches from a drawer. He understood now. She'd probably turned on the oven when the pilot had gone out and filled the kitchen with gas. She was lucky she hadn't died.

"I have a system so I don't get burnt alive," she said, as though reading his thoughts. "That isn't how I want to go." She laughed, but to herself, as if she'd told a riddle he couldn't answer.

He knelt and lit the pilot and pulled himself upright to light the stovetop. They stood together before the range, all four burners turned high, their blue flames dancing in mute ecstasy, or, if viewed another way, as souls tormented. Then he looked at her, directly for the first time, and saw the naked wish on her face. She hadn't forgotten a thing, not this woman with her systems and solitary laughter and grief. The flickering light revealed what she'd wanted all along. And, terribly, that she almost had it. The sweet rush of that knowledge filled the kitchen between them, the hiss and spit and savage bark of it.

HEADED FOR WORK
BY MOLLY O'DELL

Along Virginia Route 11, dogwoods
verge to bloom. Flashing lights
of an oncoming car warn
me to take it slow around
the next curve. Three cows
lumber across the highway.
Out-fenced. Unaware. Full.
At some point in the morning,
the farmer will notice them
gone. He'll catapult
into retrieving two blacks
and a brown. By noon,
the cows will graze
with the herd
inside a mended fence,
and the farmer will not
have accomplished one thing
he had planned for the morning.

READ THIS
(BECAUSE MY LIFE DEPENDS ON IT)
BY PRIYA KAVINA

THEY KILLED HER. If you take anything from this, let it be that the Intellectual Informatics Intelligence killed my mama. They—the I's—the Eyes—want me to believe she's still alive, that she's sitting in our family room, but that *thing* is not my mother. I don't have much time alone, so the best I can do is summarize how I know this.

That morning, before they pushed pentobarbital through her veins, Mama stuck a capsule in my mouth, in the gap my upper wisdom tooth would grow into. "Swallow this when they take you up to the seventh floor." When the Eyes deposited me in room 718 of the Families First Department and told me, "Hang on just a minute, sweetie," I pulled the dry pill onto my tongue and tried pushing it down my tightening throat. When the door opened, the pill went down with a swig of horror.

"Ready to go, Gopher?" Mama called me Gopher for the way I used to tunnel up through her sheets in the middle of the night when I got scared. I don't know why, but that morning she told me, "Gophers are a very important part of our ecosystem. They bring chaos to carefully curated gardens."

The woman standing in the doorframe looked just like her. I wanted to hug her so bad. She held out a hand and I took it, expecting the spark. Mama, the real Mama, had told me the burst of electrical signals would mess with my brain and fool me into believing this hyper-realistic humanoid robot really was my mother. Because if I believed it was my mother, so would our neighbor and the grocer, and so would you. The pill would counter my delusion. Break the chain.

The bot was so much like Mama that I almost liked cuddling up next to it. Mama's memories—the ones they deemed harmless and uniform—had been uploaded into its mainframe, so it knew I liked hot cocoa with drizzles of hazelnut. It knew I stayed late after school on Tuesdays for Coding Club. It knew where the spoons were and that we stashed a white envelope full of emergency cash in the back of the linen cabinet. But it didn't know how that scar under its left eye came about, or how my father left us because he thought Mama was a crazy conspiracy theorist. She wasn't. And neither am I. This bot is proof of that.

It nauseates me that I have to hug it and tell it *I love you* just as I would to my real mama. But everything has to look normal. It's recording me, monitoring me. Making sure I don't turn out like the inquisitive woman who raised me.

I decided I'd go along with the sham until I worked out a plan to expose the rats who destroyed my family. The task keeps me sharp and the life-like Mama keeps me from spiraling into grief. She makes me hot cocoa when she thinks I'm stressed. She asks me about my dreams and my friends at school. I've started saying *thank you* and *good morning* and *goodnight*. Then yesterday I said *I love you* without feeling like I would puke.

That's how I knew the pill was wearing off. I'm running out of time. I put this all into writing to help myself remember and to pass my story on to you.

I can't bear this secret alone. Every time I hear a knock on the door, I think it's them. Any time I feel a pinch in my body, I think it's a needle releasing a lethal dose of pentobarbital into my veins.

I don't know what Mama knew, but that doesn't matter. I just want you to believe me when I say the Eyes are killing off our loved ones and we aren't even aware of it.

A creak in the hall tells me Mama—I mean the bot—is coming to check on me. When she senses I'm scared, she brings me hot cocoa with drizzles of hazelnut. She's thoughtful that way.

WHEE...E...E
DENNIS PISZKIEWICZ

PASSPORT
BY GLEN ARMSTRONG

Note the wasteland and the harbor.
Prepare a small bundle.

Teach anyone who asks how to read.
Walk until you stumble.

Examine all motives,
particularly your own.

Question.
Some strangers here are looking

for enlightenment.
Sleep in the warehouse.

Drink water from streams.
Don't make the same mistakes

that I did years ago.
Save your sad songs

for the coffeehouse,
but don't save them forever.

ri

FUTURE ON MARS
BY BARBARA DEMARCO-BARRETT

WHEN COLTON'S WIFE Lolly ran off with Rolf, a hippie guy with young Rutger Hauer Aryan good looks, he convinced me to leave San Francisco where I'd just moved after graduating from college and come to Laguna Beach to be with him.

"For just a little while," he said. He was so broken up.

He and I had been having an affair, which Lolly mistakenly agreed to, even encouraged us to enter. It was the early '80s, a time when anything was possible, and in our circle, you were considered a prude to put on the brakes when feelings were strong.

I was as guilty as he, so I agreed.

No sooner had I arrived when he said, "I'm broker than Moses' tablets."

"Thanks for telling me," I said, as I sat on the bed and pondered the pipe as wide as a python that ran from the upstairs apartment through Colton's bedroom into the floor. Colton said it was the pipe from the neighbor's toilet. How symbolic.

Laguna was compared to the French Riviera. The beach town had cliffs where you could stand and gaze upon the turquoise water and waves crashing below. Dozens of restaurants and shops that catered to people with money. We had no money.

"You misled me," I said. "I thought it would be better than this."

"I didn't mean to pull you into a sorry-ass life," he said. "Didn't think I'd lose my job, too."

"I could use a cigarette," I said. I was smoking then, however minimally. It was an expensive habit, especially when you were broke.

He dug through his pockets and kitchen drawers for change and counted out twenty-seven cents. Enough for two Nat Shermans.

Lovely. Two cigarettes. It was something.

Nat Shermans were thin, brown-papered, expensive cigarettes sold individually beside the cash register at the Circle K. We might be poor, but we still had good taste.

The sun dribbled into the Pacific Ocean as we moseyed on foot down Glenneyre Street to the market.

Colton's wife Lolly and I had been friends in college. We'd met Colton at the same exact moment outside the cafeteria where we'd set up a table to sell our baked goods—muffins, cookies, freshly baked bread. The two of them paired up, quit school, and moved to Southern California, Colton's home. Four years later, I was back in the picture. I visited them in Laguna. Things heated up between Colton and me, but we wanted to do the right thing. We discussed our mutual attraction with Lolly before we even so much as kissed. Then, the morning I was to catch a plane home, Lolly snuck out at sunrise, taking with her all of Colton's pants, including his briefs. He slid between the sheets of the narrow futon where I slept and we made love. When she came home at dinnertime, she confessed that she left with his pants hoping we'd have sex and get over it, but our dalliance had only served to plunge us in deeper, make us think we were in love.

She said, "Go ahead, have an affair. You're so alike you'll burn each other out in seven months."

So we went ahead. But seven months later it was she who had burned out. She couldn't take it anymore and that's when she ran off with Rolf.

At the market, Colton paid for our cigarettes. We crossed PCH and strolled to the end of Thalia Street, where we smoked our Shermans and watched the sun's final descent into the Pacific.

Two weeks was up.

"I have to go home," I said, blowing smoke rings. Lolly's disappearance, along with our penniless state, had tarnished our glimmery affair.

"Just stay till I get it together," he said.

"How much longer will that be?"

"Not long," he said.

"I have a job interview in two days," I said. "I really need this job."

"You can't leave me," he said. "You're the reason my marriage got all screwed up."

"I don't recall holding a gun to your head," I said.

His jaw tightened then relaxed and he said, "You have a room up there, right? In that house on Mars Street?"

"I do," I said, fearing what was coming.

"I could come with you, right? My luck would change in Frisco."

"No one calls it Frisco except for tourists," I said.

Light had all but disappeared from the sky. A boat just beyond the shoreline drifted about, its running lights mere specks.

"A change of geography never changed anybody's luck," I said.

That made him look dejected. I felt like that boat, adrift, going nowhere in particular, with a man as rudderless as me.

Everything inside of me said, *No, don't come,* but I said, "All right." It was half my fault and I felt bad that his life was so screwed up. We had never meant for it to go this far. I hadn't, anyway.

"My lease is up at the end of the month," he said. "Only nine days away. I'll join you then."

"Sounds good," I said. "I'll go tomorrow. You come when you can."

Later that night in the bedroom, I packed. Upstairs, someone flushed the toilet and the whoosh of water rushed down the pipe past me on its way to wherever it goes. Tomorrow I'd be gone, back to an uncertain future on Mars.

ADRIFT IN EDISON

SUSAN EMERY

UNION STATION
BY MICHAEL CONLON

TWO THIN RED lines above a thicker blue run the length of each vacant silver train car. They stretch out beneath a platform roof, extending toward a spider web of tracks that leads out of Union Station. Faded concrete industrial buildings rear up behind rusted fencing topped by barbed wire guarding the railroad yard. The brown San Gabriel Mountains rise in the distance beneath an early morning grey sky.

Rich tows the black canvas suitcase behind him across the platform, a green knapsack sagging over his left shoulder. Like a stranger searching for an address on an unfamiliar street, he glances up at the numbers on each car as he passes—"39970...39971...39975." The gap in the sequencing bothers him.

He catches his image in the tinted windows of a car's double-door entrance. Visions of a fit young man with backpack, red Eurail train schedule in hand, and a glint in his eye dissolve into a stoop-shouldered man, hair tinged with gray, belly protruding above his belt, wrinkled eyes peering out behind rimmed glasses. He looks away and moves on until he spies "39977...Coast Starlight...Sonoma Valley." With no benches nearby, he sets the knapsack on top of the suitcase and leans against a metal column. The morning moon continues to fade between the gap in the platform roofs. He considers grabbing for an apple or a granola bar, then decides to wait until the train reaches the ocean at Oxnard heading toward Santa Barbara. Something to anticipate, to distract.

Behind the doors of his car, a porter in a dark cap, vest, and black tie checks a clipboard while chatting on an extended cord phone. Behind him sits the baggage storage area beneath a stairway that leads to the upper observation deck extending the full length of the car. Rich had reserved a seat on the bottom right, window facing inland.

The ground begins to vibrate as a locomotive rumbles to life, sending a shiver through Rich's chest. His throat tightens. For a moment, he wishes that this trip was ending instead of starting; that his decision to separate was for hours, not weeks; that he could be heading home to a house and the wife he once knew.

But the downstairs room at home remained vacant, no matter how many times he walked by; no matter how often he entered and sat on the bed, looking up at the pictures of a little leaguer or a junior lifeguard or a happy family snuggled in color-coordinated outfits, posed at the beginning of a school year in front of a pier at the beach. Smiling seemed so simple back then—so taken for granted. Danny's smile; Danny's hand on Rich's shoulder.

His eyes begin to sting. He cups his head in his hand, looks down, closes his eyes. He has his current wish. He is alone. No need to be somewhere; to be someone. He recalls a time he sat on a train alone, decades ago, a continent and an ocean away from loved ones and friends. Yet he had never felt so isolated, so helpless, as here, less than an hour away from home. This journey holds no possibilities; no purpose; no timetable. He only knows he will be taken away.

Voices approach. He wipes his eyes and looks up. Local commuters without reserved seats begin huddling near the sealed doors. Those who perhaps have reservations chat on the far benches. His intention is simple. He won't be talking to anyone until he reaches Davis just before midnight. He'll put his backpack on the seat next to him. If someone insists on sitting, even talking, he'll just point to his throat and rasp, "Laryngitis."

With a blast of air, the train doors part. The porter, now formal in his jacket, steps out onto the platform and smiles.

"Ladies and gentlemen, this is the Coast Starlight, destinations Santa Barbara, San Luis Obispo, Oakland, and Redding. Then, for those who dare, into the Oregon Territory and the wilderness beyond." He grins. "Those with reservations, let me know if I can be of assistance. All aboard!"

Rich waits until the crowded entrance clears. He slings the knapsack over his right shoulder with a thump, grabs the handle of his suitcase, and moves past the porter, eyes down. He crosses the small gap between platform and train, above the soiled gravel below, then lifts his suitcase to the highest section of the rack. He ducks beneath the stairs and up the aisle to find his home for the next sixteen hours.

FIRSTBORN (FOR HOLLY)
BY ELLEN GIRARDEAU KEMPLER

I still remember the indelible new of you—
the surprise of your belly-rippling kick,
my inflatable balloon-womb growing taut,

the blade of your elbow in my ribs,
the heft of your head wedged between bones,
edging inexorably down.

Waddle-walk forward to the day we met.
Your blind mouth latched on tight,
gumming hard for milk.

Sluggish in my swollen body,
starved for sleep,
I struggled to fill your searching need—

both dreading & embracing the hospital farewell,
the solemn promise of the nurse's serious joke,
"For the next eighteen years, she's yours."

FARMERS' MARKET SHOPPERS
JEREMIAH GILBERT

THAT'S ALL
BY NICOLE IM

I need to be more Korean or more white.

Like, I need to actually become fluent
in the language people assume
I can speak or track
down forgotten white ancestors
who came through Ellis Island in the 1900s.

The key to conformity is dilution.

But ancestry.com doesn't work so well
when you can't accurately spell your grandfather's name with
English letters
and you aren't quite sure
who ended up on which side after WWII.

The demarcators of the 38th parallel didn't think
to provide maps for lost descendants.

When I was a child, I told people
I was half Korean
and that's all.

ABOUT AHAB OR
SOMETHING LIKE THAT
BY EIREENE NEALAND

I DON'T KNOW if your professor is an old white dude, but mine's name is Mike, and he gave us ten essay question prompts and said five would be on the test. I took them to my tutor, and she helped me write the answers out, but I had anxiety dreams about all of it: harpoons, the coffin symbolism.

"It's too much severed head stuff."

Meanwhile, I got a lot of texting done in that class.

One day, while I was trying to send my dad a link, Professor Mike walked down the aisle and right up to me.

"If this was high school, I would take that away from you," he said, and I was like, "Yeah, but it isn't high school."

"Oh," he said. "Okay, well, sorry about that then."

"Sorry," I said, and went on with my text.

"Millie is doing fine," I wrote to my dad. "Millie"—that's me—"is fine, but she talks too much in class."

That night, when I was folding laundry in my apartment box, I told my cat how oppressive that professor had been. I mean, the nerve, the inhumanity of him, forcing me to ask for my own space. Wasn't he supposed to content himself with glaring at us from the helm? What else could he have been doing standing by me in the aisle aside from trying to look down my shirt, although everyone knows that Queequeg was tattooed, and queer, and a cannibal, despite all the bowing and incense? My tutor explained all that to me.

"I bet Professor Mike doesn't know how to assess the age of an iPhone," I told her when we sat in her little white office with no posters or even a window or light. Who was she to get so big-eyed at all the red marks on my test? "When is it fair to get another, even if the screen hasn't cracked?"

But of course she had no answer, unlike my dad who says Apple's ten-month lifespan is just a factory suggestion, while two versions back is perfectly fine as long as you buy a spot in the cloud. Anyhow, aren't I an adult now? I have a job and can go to Target and buy a pillow if I want to, or concert tickets, or tequila, or food.

Awaiting student loans, I finished off a bottle last night with Ryan, then drank so much I threw up all over his shoes. My cat threw up with me, and we lay together on the carpet in a smelly swash, looking up at the cheap perforated ceiling, contemplating where we next wanted to sail. Target, I thought, because it was my fault, the vomit and all that anxiety of my dad's.

For my birthday, I got the cat wet food and let her eat as much as she wanted, which was a mistake. She always wants more, but wet food is expensive.

"Look where it ends up," I told her as embalmed heads entered my dreams.

When I woke up, I hardly recognized anything—not even my laundry hamper, which was full of socks. That's all I ever put in there; socks, workout clothes. The floor is where I keep my outfits and various random junk that I buy, like the green cactus light I got at Target. Who needs a neon green light shaped like a cactus on the side of your makeup table? But the price tag said $7.99, so I thought, *Wow! That's a steal. I'll buy it and resell it online.* Why not, Captain A-hab? Starbuck would give a thumbs-up, even if what I realized when I got down the escalator was that someone had changed the sticker on it.

Downstairs, there were green cactus lights for $20.25 marked with a fairly obvious sign. But it wasn't me who changed the price tag, was it? I knew the checker wouldn't scrutinize what slipped by under the shuddering seas of the scanning tool. She wouldn't scrutinize it any more than I scrutinized the things that passed beneath my scanner at Lowe's. Take it please—get it out of here, Professor Mike—because it isn't my job to ponder the white spray heaving against us or whatever blubber floats underneath. I leave that to you, Professor Mike, with all your nose hairs in the front. *Hey prof,* I thought as I sailed through the checkout with my haul. *I guess you've got something to learn.*

I brought the light home, and now it's there on my floor, along with a whole lot of bills and cosmetics stolen from places where no cameras can look. "Why not," I said because, yeah, here I am with an ugly green cactus light moored up on my rug along with—let's see what else, Professor Mike—like, I've got a six-pack of Activia, for one. I was going to buy it, but I was already on antibiotics at the time, and they made me so drowsy I didn't want to get my wallet out of my purse. Anyhow, probiotics are as expensive as fuck, as in hell, Professor Mike, whales, Professor Mike, hey bud. I guess I'm smart enough to know that.

OAKLAND, AFTER HOURS
BY TRAVIS STEPHENS

People are walking around Lake Merritt,
mostly clockwise on this Tuesday. It is
early evening, after work, so the women
wear dedicated Spandex and the men
try not to notice. I am tearing the wall
out of a house my son has purchased, he
is out of town, and I wear plaster dust
atop my usual dumb look.
I work alone, with an iPod half full of
old tunes; cheap bastard I am, to not
download some more. It is a soundtrack
to the recent past, a mix of nostalgia
and pop hits. When I wasn't looking
Uncle Lonely joined me. He brought a
few cold beers, so what the hell, we
adjourn to the porch to watch women
go by. Seventy degrees outside.
The bottles leave wet circles.
Lonely let his pal Regret, dressed all
in black, come in. He brings a big

bottle of WhatIf and we pass it around.
Come to find out Lonely is a half cousin
to Distance, and a nephew of Bad Choices.
All my half-brothers.
They kid me about a bar not far, of doors that open.
Remember Michelle or Liz of twenty years ago?
The way a moon tastes in summer.
Not this moon. Another.
I sat too long.
Look, there is a chunk of wall waiting, nails to pull.
Beer is about gone so you boys either
lend a hand or go on home.
I mean it.
I am going to set up floodlights and get
serious with that hammer.

BALANCING ACT

JAMES DECHARY

TITUBA FLOATS AN EGG WHITE
BY JANE YOLEN

Her homey magic intrigues the girls.
A song in an unknown language,
wave of her dark hands
through the translucent air.
She sets an egg white
adrift in a bowl.
It floats like a compass
pointing the way to their true loves.
In such a tightly anchored world,
the drifting albumin
makes them tremble with decisions,
but they are fascinated, too.
Such is the Devi's web,
this intimate ocean,
Tituba stirs the mixture slowly
with a wooden spoon.

SORRY, MONA
BY STEVE FAYNE

THE NOTICE, SHORT and not-so-sweet, was in with my paycheck on Thursday. After thanking me for my years of service, it said that the plant would be moving offshore and my employment would terminate at the end of the month. Two weeks' notice after thirty years. Son of a bitch. I looked across at Charlie and could tell by the look on his face that he'd gotten the same news. They'd need the engineers, the mechanics, and some of the maintenance guys to dismantle and pack up the machinery, but the line guys like us, we were toast. Once they got rid of the union in '98, we had no leverage and it was all downhill. Productivity quotas increased every year and our hourly rates hardly moved at all. There was always someone new willing to work for less money and less benefits. That's what killed the union.

Who's going to hire a fifty-seven-year-old guy who doesn't know how to do anything but build refrigerators? Ours was the last appliance plant in this part of the country and they sure as hell weren't building any new ones. Thank God at least the kids were grown and on their own. It was just me and Mona, but I remortgaged the house when the kids went off to college and I've still got twenty years of payments ahead of me. Mona was going to freak out. She hadn't worked since we made the last tuition payment, and with her arthritis, there's not much chance that she could.

At the end of the shift, Charlie and I decided to have a few before we had to go home to face the wives. We'd been carpooling to work the last twenty years and he'd driven that day, so I needed to make sure he didn't get too loaded. Joe's was way more crowded than usual at the end of the shift. Looked like everyone had the same idea. We elbowed our way up to the bar, got four beers, and wandered out to what passed for a patio at Joe's. There were a couple of chairs in the corner under a half-dead oak tree, and we collapsed into them and started working on those beers.

Later, I'm not exactly sure how much later, we were both very drunk and Charlie was in no condition to drive. Joe called a cab and we stumbled into it. At home, I fumbled with my keys trying to open the door, and eventually I heard the lock click and it was pulled open from the inside. Mona. A very pissed-off Mona. How did I forget to call to tell her I'd be late?

"You're drunk."

Didn't need her to tell me. I could hardly stand up.

"Everybody's fired. Plant's moving to Mexico."

I started collecting unemployment the next week. At first I was reluctant to go down there, but then Mona reminded me that they've been taking money out of my check for years and I never used it. When I got it, I looked at the paltry amount and panicked just a bit. We didn't have a lot of savings and we weren't going to survive long on this kind of money. With Mona's help and some internet guidance, I prepared a resume that might have slightly exaggerated my experience and ability and sent copies out to every company within seventy-five miles that manufactured anything.

Most just ignored me. A few wrote back, standard letters that said, "Thanks, but no thanks."

The folks at the unemployment office claimed to have some leads and I followed up as best I could. The jobs were either already filled or paid less than unemployment. Every week, our bank balance dropped, and I had to seriously consider which bills to pay and which to hold. I walked around the house turning off lights, canceled our subscription to the paper, and gave up beer. Lost a few pounds with that one but didn't save all that much money. We started talking about selling the house, but what with the refinance and property values around here in free fall after the plant closed, even that wasn't going to help much.

Mona had been looking at apartments around town, trying to figure out if there was anything that we could afford, but I really didn't want to sell the house that I grew up in. We bought it from my folks when they retired and moved to Arizona. I wandered around from room to room, trying to think of some way to stave off the inevitable.

Of course, lots of folks around here were in the same boat, not that that made me feel any better. A lot of us picked up our checks at the same time and sat around bullshitting about our plans. None of the guys, even the young ones, had found work. A few guys moved away, hoping to find something elsewhere, but no one ever called back with good news.

Back at home, I opened my desk drawer to check my bank balance and there, under my checkbook, was my life insurance policy. I bought it when the kids were young and had been paying on it ever since.

Could I?

"Sorry, Mona. Not today."

RON

BY ELAINE BARNARD

I TRY TO get here before anyone, 7 a.m. at the latest. It's a public gym, so you never know who's gonna show up. But I like my privacy, so I try to work out without anyone staring at my leg. That is, the one that isn't there, that's attached to my thigh like a long black snake for balance. Kids are the worst. They never stop gawking. Their parents correct them, but hell, they're just kids. They can't help but stare at something so ugly, so strange.

I used to wear long pants to cover the prosthetic, but it's so damned hot in this gym that I said the hell with it. Let them stare. I'm wearing shorts. So here I am in my shorts, hoping to avoid the stares by getting here before the goons arrive.

So I'm lifting weights when this woman appears. Kinda chubby, skimpy gym attire, red bottoms, tight black top, gray ponytail. "The fans aren't on," she complains.

"I don't think we'll get that sweaty," I reply, hoping she'll forget the fans and get to her workout, leave me be with my weights.

She waddles onto a bike and starts to pedal. I used to ride bikes, rode in marathons all over California. I loved it. Loved that breeze whipping the sweat out of my eyes, cooling my muscles.

"Where's the TV remote?" she grumbles, getting off her bike and searching the equipment. "Don't you watch television while you work?"

I don't answer. Just continue to lift, heavier and heavier. I hate TV. It destroys my peace. Who wants to hear the news anyway? Never anything good, anything hopeful on CNN or NBC. Just some more news of floods and fires, sanctions on Iran or China or whomever our president decides to punish. I like silence, like the sound of myself, my grunts and groans.

"Be careful," she warns. "You could injure yourself lifting those things."

Maybe I want to injure myself. Then I'll end up where I started, back in Afghanistan on that stretcher, waiting for them to load me on that helicopter, fly me back to the States to vegetate while they decide what to do about my missing limb.

"Hey," she says, "do you have a favorite channel? Maybe I could get it for you."

I don't answer, hoping she'll get the hint.

"I like to watch the food channels," she tells me. "Appease my appetite for the day. I hate to cook, so I pretend I've made all those dishes. But I still can't lose weight."

I wish she'd shut up about weight. I've been trying to gain a few. Somehow I keep losing, losing, losing. Docs say it's nerves. "You're just a bundle of nerves, Ron."

They give me pain pills and tranquilizers, uppers and downers. I'm so mixed up with all the stuff I've ingested. The only thing seems real are these weights. I know when I lift them. I can feel the blood rush through my body, the tingle in my arms, the inhale and exhale. That's what it's all about, inhaling and exhaling, exhaling and inhaling, exhaling…

I'm climbing on my bike. It's been a long time since I've been on my bike. I need to feel the wind on my face. I start to pedal hard, faster and faster. I'm back in a marathon. My legs are strong, never been stronger. I'm ahead now. The others are trailing behind me, but they're getting close, closing in. I strain, shove my last shred of energy into it. I've come in first. I've won. My team surrounds me, lifts me on their shoulders. I gasp for breath. The weights drop from me, just missing my missing leg. I feel myself falling, falling, falling…

Through the haze, I see her kneeling beside me. Her chubby fingers wipe the sweat from my forehead. "Hang in there," she murmurs, offering me a sip from her almost empty water bottle. "They'll be here soon. They promised."

Somehow her voice calms me as we wait. Suddenly, a siren shrills the silence. An elevator thuds to a stop. Muffled voices. I remember those voices. They are lifting me . . . lifting me to their shoulders.

ft

CONSOLATION
BY TIM SUERMONDT

The star right outside my window
is pulsating with the spirit of friends,

all of them telling me not to rush,
they'll be plenty of time before I join

the endless traveling of the universe.
We remember and remember, things

of importance and things of nonsense—
one of them tells a bad joke and when

I reply with a bad joke of my own I hear
moaning and laughter as the star pulls

up and is quickly out of sight. "See you
again," I say to myself, never goodbye.

A PLACE FOR DREAMS
JENNIFER GRIFFITHS

LEAVING HOME BEHIND
BY DANIELLE DAYNEY

"SEE YOU SOON," I said to Justin, my husband, after he kissed me goodbye in Detroit. I watched him drive away from our fifth-floor window as he left for Brooklyn to establish his career and our new life together. I stayed behind in our apartment for a month to pack.

I folded my clothes and stuffed them in cardboard boxes. Long sleeves first, because it was almost summer. I packed jeans and dresses on their hangers. It would make unpacking in our new apartment easier. I left out the sweatshirt with the Old English D because I thought I might need it at night when the cool breeze bit from the Detroit River.

I wrapped the kitchen glasses in grocery bags because I couldn't afford bubble wrap or newspaper. I didn't have many pots or pans; just hand-me-downs from Mom. The thought of keeping one out crossed my mind. But I decided to live on sandwiches, salads, and cereal. It was only a month, after all. I packed the pans away and taped the box shut.

I left a few things next to the trash chute—old artwork and chairs from Ikea that wouldn't fit in the truck, the ripped Nelly Furtado hoodie that held memories of late nights and laughter in its pocket, and the S-shaped shelf that once displayed photos of friends.

Each day after work, I walked my dog Roxy around Comerica Park, recalling the way a home run echoed off my favorite player's bat. I remembered the chants for Magglio, Verlander's no-hitter, and Zumaya's wicked fastball. I asked myself if watching the Yankees would give me the same joy. Would I forget how much I loved nestling into the crowd for a Saturday night game?

One evening, I stopped in front of the gate to see the green field. Closing my eyes, I imagined the taste of a Hebrew National with just mustard and the way sweat pooled at the small of my back before the August sun would drop behind the top of the stadium. I wondered: would the sunsets look different in Brooklyn? Would the sky change from blue to pink and crimson before settling in below the trees? Would my neighborhood even have trees to look at, to breathe in autumn, to catch snow in winter, and to bloom in the spring?

A few days before the move, I invited my friends over one last time. The ones who had been there for the parties, for the fun, but also for the real moments. Anna, a girl whose hair I saved from a fire at the first Detroit party I went to. Sam, the sweet one with an infectious laugh, and Matilda, an artist from next door. We danced. We sang. We reminisced about the late-night parties in my apartment.

"No one will ever replace you guys. You are literally the best." I looked them in the eyes and promised them I would never let go, even with hundreds of miles stretching between my palms and theirs. They promised the same.

But some promises are meant to be broken.

When Justin came home, I kissed him. I hugged him, breathing his cologne. It was the one scent I could bring with me from home.

I reminded myself why we were going—his career, our future together. In the last two years, Detroit had slowly crumbled around us. The auto industry collapsed. Friends lost their jobs. If we stayed, the S-shaped shelf and happy faces in those photos would fall to dust with this city. I had to leave and salvage what was left.

I watched friends carry my blue leather couch, old dresser, and favorite vintage lamp from my apartment. One by one, they loaded them into the truck. We left the most important things behind—the skyline, my favorite bar, my friends, my heart.

Once the apartment was empty, I sat on the floor, alone, and said goodbye to what was left—the blank space, the parquet wood floors, the echo off avocado-green walls, the memories of home.

I told myself it's okay to cry.

THE SILVER THREAD
BY CHRISTINE FUGATE

I AM LYING on the floor, attempting to meditate. My BFF Lucy gave me the Calm app for my birthday. Guru Marc whispers, "One's soul can rise above the body. A silver thread tethers them together, so your soul doesn't drift away."

Sounds exciting, but nothing is happening. That's the Calm app's favorite word: nothing. Breathe in. Think a thought. Then go to nothing.

I can't even breathe correctly, much less find a silver thread. My uncle said he drifted above his body when he did a past-life acupuncture workshop with Shirley MacLaine. Grandmother paid $15,000 for that little extravaganza and Mom about shit a brick. Grandfather bought her a fur coat for Christmas that year.

I laugh over the Shirley MacLaine fur that Mom never wore. My breathing relaxes. I open my eyes, startled to be so close to the ceiling.

Holy shit! My soul is floating above the green velvet couch. My Persian cat stares at something right below me. I roll over to see if it's my silver thread. There's only my body lying on my deep red rug.

That's when I notice my hair's new golden streaks. I wanted pink tones like Harley in *Suicide Squad*, but my sensible hairdresser vetoed that idea.

Oh God. I'm climbing higher, drifting towards the open window. My lungs tighten as panic replaces oxygen.

"Breathe in, breathe out," Guru Marc says.

Rays of sunlight highlight my bare, hairy legs. My dress has baby's breath flowers printed on it, like the ones I had in my wedding bouquet. Pure and fragile with strong stems. When I reached the altar, Tom had whispered, "You are a baby's breath of fresh air."

I'm about to hit the ceiling fan. Can a soul be chopped up into tiny pieces, or does it merely float through the blades? Terror squeezes my heart. I need my inhaler before my asthma kicks in.

In through the nostrils, out through the mouth. Thank God. The vice grip on my lungs loosens.

My princess-cut diamond sparkles rainbows all over the walls. Why am I wearing my wedding ring? Think. Go to fucking nothing.

Nothing. Nothing.

Tom moved back into the house yesterday. The day before my twenty-ninth birthday. He begged for forgiveness over his lies and that bitchy paralegal in his office. Tears rolled down his face as he apologized. I cried, too. Four years I waited for that apology.

Lucy would not be happy. She doesn't understand my stress. Ever since Mom died, farm paperwork is all I do. I don't know how Mom dealt with all the soybeans, cows, and corn inventory.

Now I need Tom to take care of selling the land. And he needs me. Or at least that's what he said.

My stomach growls like a ravenous dog. I never ate lunch. I hear footsteps on the stairs.

"Honey, can you please help me?" My body smashes against the ceiling. "Tom!" I scream.

Nothing from Tom. He's gone into his office. Damn paperwork.

"Sweetheart, I'm done meditating. I seriously need your help."

He walks into the living room and stares at me, lying on the floor.

"Tom, I'm up here." I wave my arms around like a crazy woman. He pulls out his beloved phone and walks back into his office. Doesn't he know I can hear? He must think my headphones are on.

"Lucy," he says, "I'll be over around six."

Are they throwing me a surprise party?

He laughs. "Alright, keep the bubbly on ice."

Tom knows I hate champagne. This can't be right.

"Just getting the paperwork together so I can file tomorrow."

File! What the hell? "Tom, I can't do this again," I cry. "You promised me no more affairs." My face boils hot.

The asshole chuckles as he walks back into the living room with an overstuffed Tumi briefcase—the one I got him for our second anniversary.

"There's nothing funny about this. I am separated from my body. Look at me!"

He takes out his handkerchief and blows his nose. I reach for his curly blond hair but he walks swiftly towards the back door. I move my arms in a freestyle stroke but my spirit doesn't budge.

The door slams. My soul plunges, hovering right above my baby's breath dress. Now I see it. Of course. That stupid silver thread is wrapped around my neck.

Guru Marc murmurs, "Namaste."

I cannot breathe.

I go to nothing.

WE WERE THREE WOMEN IN A CITY OF WATER (LIVING AGAIN)

BY PATRICIA BASSEL

At first we were heavy with talk of work and wanting,
but with every corner turned we became lighter with rhapsody.
We left behind stories that shaped our desire,

stories of dry prairie winds and the need for rain,
of western sunlight that warms the skin of dark scars—
to see what lies ahead on the broken cobblestones of Venice

where still rule the old, the aged—
where youth is on the other side of the bridge.
As we stepped through the narrow passageway of rare friendships,

we smiled, we sipped prosecco, we ate gelato—
stracciatella, castagna, frutti di bosco.
We mingled with the ghosts of countless Venetian lovers.

We were three women in a city of water
where the trickle of laughter seeps down the stone through the ages
and youth is on the other side of the bridge.

A SEARCH FOR THE PERFECT MEAL FROM HOME

BY JEAN HASTINGS ARDELL

I'M OLD ENOUGH to know that Thomas Wolfe was right—once you've left you can't go home again—not in the sense of slipping back into the comfort of the way things were. But I'm also gullible enough to believe that you can reinvent a bit of home wherever you find yourself. And it's funny the small things you took for granted growing up that loom large in memory as the years pass in the town you now call home, leaving you caught between two loved places.

I was born in Brooklyn, grew up in Queens, and went to school in Manhattan. By the time I was a teenager, I knew I wanted to live in California, where I'd heard you could ride horses on the beach. And so it was that I ultimately came to Laguna Beach and settled down happily, though horseless. I loved the unfamiliar cuisine: tacos, guacamole, sautéed abalone garnished with almonds. But each summer I came to crave a meal of Maine lobster. Just the line on a menu, "Live Maine lobster!" was enough to launch a powerful longing. (The "live" referred to the lobsters that were transported alive in their seawater till you ordered one up.)

The problem was, in California, live Maine lobster is considered a delicacy, served in fine restaurants with white linen tablecloths. There is no way to dine on lobster with elegance, unless the staff does the heavy labor of cracking the shells and extracting the meat from within. But the process is part of the fun, and besides, such elegance is the antithesis of my experience back East, when going for lobster meant a trip to the beach, where you dined in casual comfort, sometimes within sight of the lobster traps bobbing in the cove. You'd sit under a ramada at wooden tables that were often unsteady, with checkered paper napkins and often newspapers used as tablecloths. The lobster was served with corn on the cob and coleslaw and, of course, melted lemon butter. Such a meal represented the essence of summer to me—relaxed and of the ocean.

Imagine my delight, then, when I learned of a restaurant up the coast that ran Monday night specials of live Maine lobster for...$9.99. You were urged to arrive early, before the supply ran out. I shared the news with my husband, a guy always game for an adventure, and two nonagenarian local friends who had lived in Manhattan for years before settling in Laguna Beach in 1955. They were game, too.

And so it was that we drove north on Coast Highway to the restaurant in a place called Pacific City in Huntington Beach. The valet parked our car ($8.00) and we entered a rustic open space with the large doors flung wide to the ocean breeze. Just across the highway was the beach. Wooden tables and chairs. Paper napkins. The cheerful waiter took our order, and one by one the plates of lobster appeared.

The lobsters were small, probably barely over the size minimum below which they cannot be harvested; the melted butter was there, along with a slice of lemon. Coleslaw had to be ordered separately and corn on the cob was not on the menu. The lobster didn't taste as though it had been alive any time recently. It sat there sadly on its paper plate, a testament to the passage of time and the changes that come with it.

Still, we carried on, smiling and making the small talk—politics, baseball, travel—that makes dining out with our friends so enjoyable. But we didn't linger. As we left, I felt even more displaced. Pacific City, a recently developed commercial plaza, had little of the flavor of old Surf City, as Huntington Beach was known. The nearby apartments were advertised as "leasable luxury," likely unaffordable for any youthful surfers who sought to live within earshot of the waves. On the way home to Laguna, we realized we were still hungry and stopped for some gelato, though no amount of ice cream was going to fill my existential hunger.

Later, my pragmatic husband asked whether I was disappointed.

"Mightily," I answered.

"But what did you expect for $9.99?" he responded.

There was no good answer to this, but it was clear that I had expected too much. Time to accept that I had left my native New York and get over it. Time to go get a Wahoo's fish taco.

ALOHA, MAKENA

AMY FRANCIS DECHARY

SS BLUEBERRY
BY BLAKE REEMTSMA

My blueberry this morning
says it's Made in Chile,
which makes me wonder,
here in Los Angeles, about
distances. How did this blueberry,
in its own small sea of milk
on my spoon, make it from
South to North America?
By slow boat, I assume,
although you left my life forever
just yesterday speeding
through the Central Valley
that probably has blueberries
growing somewhere.

I imagine a ship
loaded down with blueberries
motoring north from Santiago
or west from the port
of Bakersfield. It is blueberry-colored
and named the *SS Blueberry*.
The captain, drunk on blueberry wine,
is dreaming right now
of meeting you on a beach
somewhere never invented.

I try dreaming away from you
here as if I'm still
in the same place. I am. And
I'm not. But I like how quickly
we recover our balance—
slipping unexpectedly on a wet spot
on the floor, for example,
but saving ourselves
with a spidery quickness.
That's what you are doing
right now in the rainforests
of San Francisco—saving yourself
for the captain of a blueberry
tanker. I try saving
my own self here
and seem to be succeeding
in a blueberry sort of way.
I hear laughing and drinking
in the bars and on the beaches,
and I know I am learning
how to love just enough.

THE MAN FROM THE SKY
BY JASON GAIDIS

I WOKE UP to the sound of thunder overhead. Every time we heard this thunder, Mother and Father always said something about the "allied." Then the thunder would get loud and the ground would shake.

We lived outside of the town of Carentan and whenever the thunder started, everyone turned off their house lights and turned on big lights that pointed toward the clouds. Then the lightning flashed. My five-year-old mind raced at the prospect of seeing lightning up close, before Mother and Father made us go the kitchen cellar, where food was stored.

This night, I moved out of bed as quietly as possible, crept past my parents' door, and did not let the patio door make noise behind me. I looked up to the clouds as the first big thunders began to shake the ground. Lightning flashed in the clouds and streaked from the ground to the sky. I hopped up and down and clapped my hands. I was so excited to see what my parents wouldn't let me see!

That was when I noticed other clouds. Clouds that started tiny and slowly grew. Hundreds of them all over. They were round, not fluffy like clouds normally are.

The clouds landed on the ground all around me. Men dangled from them by ropes. Fast pops sounded in the woods. Streaks of lightning flew by my head and smashed into our house.

A man tackled me to the ground. I didn't know where he came from, so I kicked and screamed and tried to get away, but he was too big. The pops became louder, then other pops sounded from the far side of our house. It was so loud that I couldn't hear anything else. It hurt my ears.

The man on top of me was yelling, but I couldn't understand what he was saying. He talked funny. He didn't talk like the mean people—the ones with red arm bands who took my friends away. This man talked like he was busy, but not mean.

Suddenly, I could feel tiny puffs all around us, like someone was throwing lots of pebbles. He pushed my head tight to the ground with his elbow and lay on top of me as he fired his gun in the direction of the woods. A few seconds later, I heard the man's gun make a ping sound. He stopped firing.

A big plane crashed in the field on the other side of the stream. The ground under us bounced up like a spring bed and fire jumped into the sky, going higher than I ever climbed in a tree. The man flipped over and lay next to me as he reloaded his gun.

I got my first look of the man in the firelight. The man had black paint streaks on his face and wore a green helmet with fishnet on it. He had lots of tools strapped to his body and the patch on his shoulder was the head of a bird.

The man from the sky looked behind me at our house, then back at me, then back at the woods, then back at me.

He jumped to his feet, scooped me up with one arm, and kicked the screen door. It broke off its hinges and flew into the kitchen. He dropped me in front of the stove and knelt down beside me. It was quieter now, but the ground still shook with thunder and the loud pops outside.

"*Mére et pére?*" the man yelled, then stood up and fired his gun out the kitchen window. The explosions from his gun shook my head and my hands over my ears didn't help. Then came the ping sound from his gun and he knelt back down.

"*Famille!*" He put more bullets into his gun. "*Où est votre famille*, kid?"

Across the kitchen, the door to the cellar burst open and my father stepped out with his pistol aimed at the man from the sky.

"*Merde!*" The man from the sky shoved me toward my father, who pulled me down the stairs to the cellar. I looked back into the kitchen before the door closed, but the man from the sky was already outside, running towards the pops and the lightning.

WHEN YOU BREAK YOUR GLASSES
BY LOJO SIMON

While putting together a mail-order desk
made in Thailand, you feel old.
You can't see the instructions:
a broken jumble of words
(affix A to by 4-C for connect side).
You fumble forward with the wrench
(in tools provided) blindly
aligning angles with alien bolts.
You flounder with the hex key
feeling this way and that
to ensure its entry—if only
sex were this straightforward
when your parts need lubrication
and his need a hand to slip inside you.

NEXT TIME

BY AMY FRANCIS DECHARY

JENNY LEFT HER beat-up Volvo next to the "Park at Your Own Risk" sign and limped in her too-tight pumps to the annual Little League Fiesta Night. A cool evening breeze blanketed the ballpark in a haze of BBQ smoke. Where was Toby? She scanned the inflatable slides, chili cookoff contest, and balloon-lined field. No sign of her son.

"You're late." A finger poked her back. "Where's my jersey?" Toby licked a giant tuft of cotton candy off a paper cone.

Damn. The jersey. "Sorry, honey," Jenny sighed. "I had an interview. There wasn't time to go home."

"I'm the only kid who doesn't have one!"

"I'll do better next time, okay?"

"When's Dad gonna be here?" Toby frowned. He'd been curt and sulking ever since the divorce.

She hadn't heard from Nick. "Soon." Tiny stars swam before her eyes and she steadied herself on the boy's shoulder. Had she eaten lunch? No, she had forgotten that, too.

A blur of green jerseys—Toby's teammates—raced by. Toby shrugged her off and ran after them. "Remember—you promised to do the Moms' Home Run Derby!"

Jenny eyed her ivory slacks and heels. *Damn. The Home Run Derby.* She started when her phone pinged in her pocket—maybe it was her recruiter Lisa with good news.

Hey babe.

Jenny rolled her eyes at her ex-husband's text. "I'm not your babe anymore, Nick," she said through gritted teeth.

Running late. Florist crisis.

69

A flush crept up Jenny's neck. He'd miss Fiesta Night for the third year in a row. He'd always been stuck at work or, as she had eventually discovered, stuck in Tiffany's bed.

The phone pinged again.

Can you pick up Toby's tux tomorrow? Tiff has to meet with the DJ.

Her face burned. First, the affair. Then, the divorce. Now, he expected her to run his wedding errands?

Jenny's cell dinged a third time. What else did he want? But it wasn't Nick. It was Lisa, checking in.

How was the meeting?

Great! Jenny replied, adding a smiley face emoji.

Knew you'd knock it out of the park!

She'd knocked it all right—accidentally knocked the HR director's coffee across the conference table. After she'd called the CEO Claire instead of Blaire.

Before she could respond to Lisa, another text popped up.

BTW, Toby needs a haircut. Thx babe.

"Ugh!" Jenny began to type a sharp retort. Her fingers, however, froze at Lisa's next message.

Just heard from Blaire. She's passing. Better luck next time.

Jenny's stomach twisted.

Call ASAP to discuss new strategy.

She jammed the phone in her purse. Ten interviews and nothing to show for it. She was out of strategies, and she was exhausted, exhausted by the fruitless interviews, making excuses for Nick, forgetting everything. She felt like those red balloons on the fence, bobbing up and down, drifting side to side, and never getting anywhere.

A voice came over the loudspeaker. "It's time for the Home Run Derby!"

While the phone jingled in the depths of her handbag, Jenny yanked off her pumps and stormed onto the field.

"Tux altered," she muttered, grabbing the longest, heaviest bat and pushing past the other Derby moms. "Florist crisis."

The buzz of the crowd drowned out the incessant chiming echoing through her brain. "New strategy," she mumbled.

The pitcher threw the ball and Jenny swung hard, so hard that the bat's weight spun her around in a circle as the ball whizzed by untouched. Laughs from the Derby moms erupted behind her. Out of the corner of her eye, she saw Toby scowling in the dugout.

Focus. She tightened her grip and the ball zipped towards her. With a metallic clink, she popped it deep into right field.

Toby pressed his nose against the dugout fencing. "You got this, Mom!"

The breeze stopped, stilling the balloons. Beyond the outfield, Nick's white Tesla glided like a ghost into an empty spot next to her Volvo. *Way to show up.* Rage flowed from Jenny's gut through her arms and legs to the tips of her fingers and toes. She dug her heels into the clay and imagined her anger seeping from her bare feet into the ground. She felt it scorch the dirt and melt through bedrock until it tapped into the Earth's fiery core.

"Didn't you read the sign, Nick?" she whispered.

The ball approached and Jenny nailed it with a sharp crack that reverberated through the stands.

"Park at your own risk."

Sparks showered home plate, and a trail of golden flames lit up the dusk as the ball sailed over the grass diamond. It soared past the balloons and into the parking lot, where it landed with a tinkling crash in the middle of Nick's windshield.

"Out-of-the-park home run!" Toby screamed over the cheers of the crowd and the blare of the Tesla's security alarm.

"Out of the park." Jenny dropped the bat in disbelief.

A gust of wind blew across the field, freeing a single balloon from its tether and floating it over a glowering Nick and the shattered glass. Jenny watched it fly away. She'd call Lisa tomorrow. She couldn't give up. She wouldn't.

"You killed it!!" Toby's sticky hand squeezed her palm. The balloon was nothing more than a dot in the new night sky. "But you also killed Dad's car."

Jenny smiled. "Better luck next time."

CODA

WORKS BY GENRE

FICTION

The Blue Flame — Lee Thomas
READ THIS (because my life depends on it) — Priya Kavina
Union Station — Michael Conlon
About Ahab or Something Like That — Eireene Nealand
Sorry, Mona — Steve Fayne
Ron — Elaine Barnard
The Silver Thread — Christine Fugate
The Man from the Sky — Jason Gaidis
Next Time — Amy Francis Dechary

NONFICTION

Fishtail Braid — Anne Gudger
Future on Mars — Barbara DeMarco-Barrett
Leaving Home Behind — Danielle Dayney
A Search for the Perfect Meal from Home — Jean Hastings Ardell

POETRY

Recalculating — James Broschart
If I Lose Myself Again — Anthony DiPietro
Headed for Work — Molly O'Dell
Passport — Glen Armstrong
Firstborn (for Holly) — Ellen Girardeau Kempler
That's All — Nicole Im
Oakland, After Hours — Travis Stephens
Tituba Floats an Egg White — Jane Yolen

CONTRIBUTORS

Jean Hastings Ardell is the author of *Breaking into Baseball* and the co-author of *Making My Pitch*. She leads memoir workshops and works as a writer and editor in Laguna Beach.

Glen Armstrong holds a Master of Fine Arts in English from the University of Massachusetts, Amherst and teaches writing at Oakland University in Rochester, Michigan. He edits the poetry journal *Cruel Garters* and has two new chapbooks: *Simpler Times* and *Staring Down Miracles*. His work has appeared in *Poetry Northwest, Conduit,* and *Cream City Review.*

Elaine Barnard's collection of stories, *The Emperor of Nuts*, was published in 2018 by New Meridian Arts. She recently won first place in the Strand's International Flash Fiction Competition. Her work has been published in numerous literary journals.

Patricia Bassel is a French/English teacher, traveler, and poet from Southwest Oklahoma. Walking is a ritual for her around the world. She connects to a place by making the most interesting discoveries on foot, even in her own neighborhood when she walks her French poodle Willie.

James Broschart is retired from classroom teaching, public television production, technical writing, and bookstore management. His poems have appeared in *Alternating Current, Amsterdam Quarterly, Ars Medica, Artemis,* and *Sociological Origins*. In 2018, Finishing Line Press published a collection of his poetry, *Old News*.

Michael Conlon, a retired high school English teacher, currently tutors students in the AVID program at San Clemente High School. He has published essays in *Orange Coast Magazine, Los Angeles Times Magazine,* and *The Orange County Register.* "Union Station" is the opening chapter of his novel in progress, *Tracks.*

Danielle Dayney is sometimes a blogger, usually a writer, and always Mom. Her stories have been published in *Beach Reads: Lost and Found,* the *VWC Centennial Anthology,* and *Nevertheless, We Persisted.* You can find her chasing kids and furbabies in Virginia or at www.danielledayney.com.

James Dechary is a student from Laguna Beach, California, where he spends his free time playing jazz, hitting tennis balls, and taking photos.

Amy Francis Dechary spent many happy years attending Laguna Beach Little League's Fiesta Night celebration. She now spends her free time watching her children play tennis, revising her novel, and leading Third Street Writers. She has never hit a home run.

Barbara DeMarco-Barrett's work has appeared in *Belle Ombre, Shotgun Honey, Cutbank, Inlandia, Los Angeles Review of Books*, and more. She runs writers retreats in Palm Springs and teaches at Saddleback College's Emeritus Institute and Gotham Writers Workshop and holds private workshops. She hosts *Writers on Writing,* KUCI-FM, and is editor of the upcoming *Palm Springs Noir* (Akashic), to be published in late 2020/early 2021.

A gay writer from Rhode Island, **Anthony DiPietro** serves as associate director of Rose Art Museum in Boston. He earned a Master of Fine Arts at Stony Brook. His writing appears in *Notre Dame Review, Spillway*, and others, including his web site, AnthonyWriter.com.

Susan Emery is an Irvine resident and mom to three young adults and one new grandchild. After working in local government for over 35 years, she retired in 2017 to pursue new interests and hobbies, primarily learning photography.

Award-winning artist **Dorothy Englander** lives and works in Albany, New York. Her art is in many public, corporate, and private collections. She holds a Bachelor of Science in art from Skidmore College and a Master of Fine Arts from the University at Albany, New York.

Steve Fayne is a mostly retired entertainment lawyer living in Laguna Beach with his wife and dogs. His previous publications were primarily covering legal issues in the entertainment business.

Christine Fugate experienced a silver thread while meditating in a Thai monastery. When not writing, Christine teaches filmmaking as an Assistant Professor at the Dodge College of Film and Media Arts at Chapman University.

Jason Gaidis holds a degree in psychology from Purdue University and a Master of Fine Arts in literary fiction from Ashland University.

Jeremiah Gilbert is an award-winning photographer and avid traveler. His photography has been published internationally and exhibited worldwide. His hope is to inspire those who see his work to discover beauty in unusual and unexpected places. He can be found on Instagram @jg_travels.

Jennifer Griffiths has worked as a fine art/commercial photographer/painter for forty plus years. Her work is in the collections of the Los Angeles County Museum of Art, the Laguna Art Museum, and the Laguna Festival of the Arts. She has taught at several colleges. Her exhibition resume is found at jennifergriffiths.me.

Anne Gudger is an essay and memoir writer who asks questions, writes hard, and loves harder. She lives in Portland. Previous work can be found at *Real Simple Magazine, The Rumpus, Slippery Elm, Tupelo Press, Atticus Review,* and *Timberline Review, Winning Writers,* and elsewhere. Her essays have won prizes from *Hippocampus, New Millennium Writings,* and *Willamette Writers.*

A graduate of the New School, **Nicole Im** holds a Master of Fine Arts in creative nonfiction. Her work has appeared in *Freeman's, Literary Hub, The Huffington Post, Hinterland Magazine,* and *Pigeon Pages.*

Priya Kavina is a creative writer who encourages you to question norms. With a passion for writing and a degree in cognitive science, she is interested in the diverse perspectives of nature, art, and science to understand societal cognition.

Ellen Girardeau Kempler's award-winning poems, essays, and articles have been widely published in print and online. Her chapbook *Thirty Views of a Changing World: Haiku + Photos* (Finishing Line Press, 2017) was praised as "a…powerful selection of climate poetics."

Eireene Nealand's stories, poems and translations have appeared in *Chicago Quarterly, The St. Petersburg Review, eohippus, WHR,* and *elimae.* She has won a Fulbright Fellowship, an Elizabeth Kostova Fellowship, an Ivan Klima Fellowship, and an Honorable Mention for the 2018 Pushcart Prize. She lives in El Granada, California.

Molly O'Dell lives, works, and writes in Southwest Virginia. Her poems and essays have been published in regional and national literary and medical journals, and her chapbook *Off the Chart* was published in 2015.

Dennis Piszkiewicz had a long career as a teacher and scientist. Along the way, he began writing. He started with a textbook and followed it with a few more books on historical topics that grabbed his interest. When not writing, he likes to explore Laguna Beach, camera in hand.

A student by day and an artist by night, **Alexandra Prado** uses art to discover and create communities. You can view her portfolio at www.alexandraprado.com and on Instagram @alexandraslens.

Blake Reemtsma is a recent graduate of Warren Wilson College's Master of Fine Arts Program for Writers and the Bread Loaf School of English. Blake is currently at work on *The Desert Geography of Love City*, his first book-length poetry collection.

Lojo Simon is a playwright, dramaturge, and Literary Laureate in Laguna Beach, California. You can learn more about her and her work at www.lojosimon.com.

Travis Stephens is a tugboat captain who resides with his family in California. A graduate of University of Wisconsin-Eau Claire, his recent credits include: *Gyroscope Review, 2River, Gravitas, Sheila-Na-Gig, Raw Art Review, Crosswinds Poetry Journal, Tiny Seed Literary Journal, Cirque, Sky Island Journal,* and *The Dead Mule School of Southern Literature.*

Tim Suermondt is the author of five full-length collections of poems, the latest being *Josephine Baker Swimming Pool* (MadHat Press, 2019). He has published in *Poetry, Ploughshares, Prairie Schooner, The Georgia Review, Bellevue Literary Review, Stand Magazine, december magazine,* and *Plume,* among many others. He lives in Cambridge, Massachusetts, with his wife, the poet Pui Ying Wong.

Lee Thomas has written for *The New York Times, The San Francisco Chronicle, Fiction Writers Review,* and elsewhere. She has fiction in *The New Guard* and *The Hopkins Review* and won the 2019 Hal Prize in the *Peninsula Pulse.* More about her work can be found at leethomaswriter.com.

Jane Yolen is the author of 382 books, all but four published by traditional publishers. She was the first woman to give the Andrew Lang Lecture in St. Andrews University in Scotland since the series began in 1927, the first writer to win the New England Public Radio Arts & Humanities Award, and the recipient of honorary doctorates by six colleges and universities for her body of work.

ACKNOWLEDGMENTS

In memory of Ned Rodriguez
(May 11, 1938 ~ June 14, 2019)

Established in 2015, Third Street Writers fosters the growth of literary arts in Laguna Beach, California. Third Street promotes the development of new and veteran writers by providing opportunities to study, produce, and celebrate all forms of literature.

Third Street Writers extends heartfelt thanks to:

- Its founding and current members
- The Laguna Beach Branch, Orange County Public Libraries
- The City of Laguna Beach 2020 Cultural Arts Funding Grant
- Laguna Beach Books
- Laguna College of Art & Design Gallery
- Laguna Beach Arts Alliance
- Laguna Beach Farmers' Market

For more information, visit our website:
www.thirdstreetwriters.org

Follow us on Instagram @thirdstreetwriters

Made in the USA
Middletown, DE
27 March 2021